BRUSH YOUR GRIZZLY BEAR GRIN

By DAVID I. A. MASON

Illustrated by DAN WIDDOWSON

CANTATA
LEARNING

MANKATO, MINNESOTA

WWW.CANTATALEARNING.COM

CANTATA LEARNING

MANKATO, MINNESOTA

Published by Cantata Learning
1710 Roe Crest Drive
North Mankato, MN 56003
www.cantatalearning.com

Library of Congress Control Number: 2014957037
978-1-63290-290-0 (hardcover/CD)
978-1-63290-442-3 (paperback/CD)
978-1-63290-484-3 (paperback)

Brush Your Grizzly Bear Grin by David I. A. Mason
Illustrated by Dan Widdowson

Book design, Tim Palin Creative
Editorial direction, Flat Sole Studio
Executive musical production and direction, Elizabeth Draper
Music arranged and produced by Mark Oblinger

Printed in the United States of America.

VISIT

WWW.CANTATALEARNING.COM/ACCESS-OUR-MUSIC

TO SING ALONG TO THE SONG

Brushing your teeth gets rid of **plaque**.

Plaque can lead to **cavities**, which hurt!

Most dentists say to brush your teeth

for two minutes twice a day.

Now turn the page,
and sing along.

Brushing your teeth is so good for your health.

It's easy to do, so just try it yourself.

Having clean teeth can be such a **delight**.

So brush, brush, brush every morning and night!

So brush your grizzly-bear grin.

Scrub that crocodile smile.

Clean those chimpanzee **chompers**.

Polish your tiger teeth.

First you **squeeze** toothpaste out onto your brush.

Careful! Take your time. There's no need to rush.

Brush in small circles to make your smile bright.

Then brush, brush, brush every morning and night!

So brush your grizzly-bear grin.

Scrub that crocodile smile.

Clean those chimpanzee chompers.

Polish your tiger teeth.

Ch ch-ch-ch ch ch ch.

Ch ch-ch-ch ch ch ch.

Ch ch-ch-ch ch ch ch.

Ch ch ch ch!

Ch ch–ch–ch ch ch ch.

Ch ch–ch–ch ch ch ch.

Ch ch–ch–ch ch ch ch!

Swish, swish, swish, spit!

Brushing your teeth at least two times a day
will help to keep those cavities away.

Cleaning your teeth keeps them **healthy** and white.
So brush, brush, brush every morning and night!

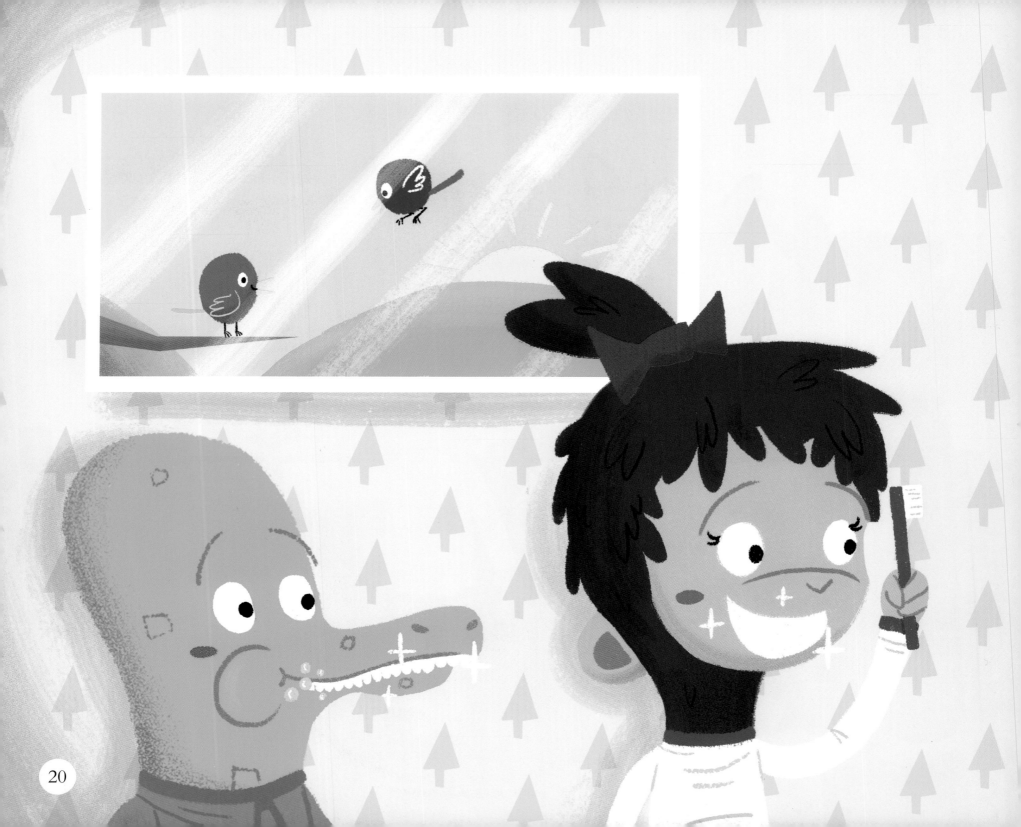

So brush your grizzly-bear grin.

Scrub that crocodile smile.

Clean those chimpanzee chompers.

Polish your tiger teeth.

SONG LYRICS
Brush Your Grizzly Bear Grin

Brushing your teeth is so good for your
  health.
It's easy to do, so just try it yourself.

Having clean teeth can be such a delight.
So brush, brush, brush every morning and
  night!

So brush your grizzly-bear grin.
Scrub that crocodile smile.

Clean those chimpanzee chompers.
Polish your tiger teeth.

First you squeeze toothpaste out onto your
  brush.
Careful! Take your time. There's no need to
  rush.

Brush in small circles to make your smile
  bright.
Then brush, brush, brush every morning and
  night!

So brush your grizzly-bear grin.
Scrub that crocodile smile.

Clean those chimpanzee chompers.
Polish your tiger teeth.

Ch ch-ch-ch ch ch ch.
Ch ch-ch-ch ch ch ch.
Ch ch-ch-ch ch ch ch.
Ch ch ch ch!

Ch ch-ch-ch ch ch ch.
Ch ch-ch-ch ch ch ch.
Ch ch-ch-ch ch ch ch!
Swish, swish, swish, spit!

Brushing your teeth at least two times a day
will help to keep those cavities away.

Cleaning your teeth keeps them healthy and
  white.
So brush, brush, brush every morning and
  night!

So brush your grizzly-bear grin.
Scrub that crocodile smile.

Clean those chimpanzee chompers.
Polish your tiger teeth.

Brush Your Grizzly Bear Grin

Tin Pan Alley
Mark Oblinger

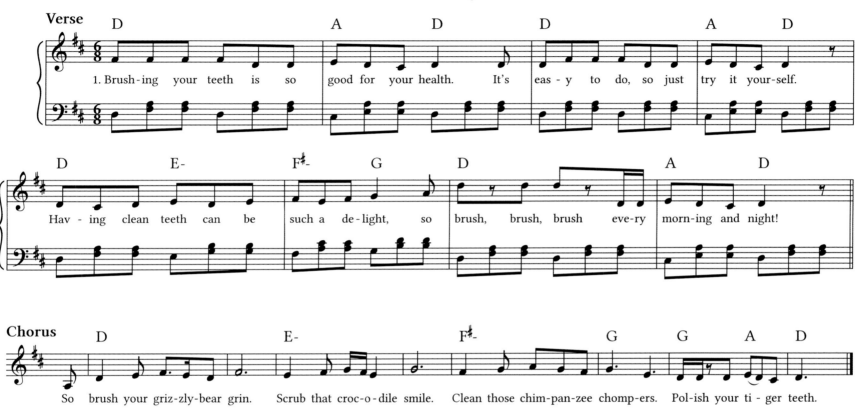

Verse

1. Brush-ing your teeth is so good for your health. It's eas-y to do, so just try it your-self.

Hav - ing clean teeth can be such a de - light, so brush, brush, brush eve-ry morn-ing and night!

Chorus

So brush your griz-zly-bear grin. Scrub that croc-o-dile smile. Clean those chim-pan-zee chomp-ers. Pol-ish your ti - ger teeth.

Verse 2
First you squeeze toothpaste out onto your brush.
Careful! Take your time. There's no need to rush.
Brush in small circles to make your smile bright.
Then brush, brush, brush every morning and night!

Chorus

Ch ch-ch-ch ch ch ch.
Ch ch-ch-ch ch ch ch.
Ch ch-ch-ch ch ch ch.
Ch ch ch ch!

Ch ch-ch-ch ch ch ch.
Ch ch-ch-ch ch ch ch.
Ch ch-ch-ch ch ch ch!
Swish, swish, swish, spit!

Verse 3
Brushing your teeth at least two times a day
will help to keep those cavities away.
Cleaning your teeth keeps them healthy and white.
So brush, brush, brush every morning and night!

Chorus

GLOSSARY

cavities—holes in teeth caused by tooth decay

chompers—another word for "teeth"

delight—a great feeling of happiness

healthy—fit and well, not sick

plaque—a coating on teeth that has tiny living things in it

squeeze—to press something firmly together

swish—to move water around in your closed mouth

GUIDED READING ACTIVITIES

1. How long should you brush your teeth? How many times a day should you brush?

2. Why is it important to brush your teeth? What are cavities?

3. What tools do you need to brush your teeth? Draw a picture of your toothbrush. What color is your toothbrush? What color is your toothpaste?

TO LEARN MORE

Dahl, Michael. *Pony Brushes His Teeth*. Mankato, MN: Picture Window Books, 2010.

Gogerly, Liz. *Teeth*. New York: Crabtree Pub., 2009.

Royston, Angela. *Why Do I Brush My Teeth?* Irvine, CA: QEB, 2009.

Smith, Siân. *Caring For Your Teeth*. Chicago: Heinemann Library, 2013.